FlannelGraphs

Flannel Board Fun for Little Ones
Preschool–Grade 3

by Jean Stangl

Fearon Teacher Aids
a division of
David S. Lake Publishers
Belmont, California

Editorial director: Ina Tabibian
Development editor: Emily Hutchinson
Production editor: Stephen Feinstein
Designer and illustrator: Walt Shelly
Design director: Eleanor Mennick
Manufacturing director: Casimira Kostecki

Entire contents copyright © 1986 by David S. Lake
Publishers, 19 Davis Drive, Belmont, CA 94002.
Permission is hereby granted to reproduce designated
materials in this book for noncommercial classroom
and individual use.

ISBN 0-8224-3060-6

Library of Congress Catalog Card Number: 85-80253

Printed in the United States of America

1 9 8 7 6 5 4 3 2 1

Contents

Introduction

A flannel graph is a board covered with felt or flannel, on which cutouts representing characters or objects are placed. It is a useful and important visual aid for presenting information, telling stories, and clarifying concepts.

Flannel graphs stimulate the imagination and attract and hold the attention of children. Most children learn through visual stimulation, and flannel graphs help them retain more information. The added tactile experience of the cutouts provides an additional sensory dimension. Auditory skills, sequencing skills, and oral language skills are also improved through flannel graph presentations.

Children will develop verbal language skills by participating in group stories and rhymes, and they will develop math readiness skills through exercises in grouping and counting. Having children place the figures on the board at the appropriate time allows for individual involvement.

For the teacher, the flannel graph can also be a valuable tool for introducing concepts of health, safety, and nutrition. For the student, it becomes a pathway for creating, discovering, and reinforcing. By placing figures on the felt board, the young child develops eye-hand coordination. Participating in adding and removing colorful figures will improve short attention spans. Through this involvement, both the restless child and the withdrawn child will be better able to cope with their behavior problems. Children can overcome self-consciousness while using the flannel graphs and figures for self-expression. Seeing the story sequence can aid the disorganized child, and the uncooperative child will discover flannel graphs to be a cooperative activity. The self-centered child will come to know the pleasure of sharing.

Older students can construct their own characters and develop short oral stories, make lesson presentations, and devise games.

Flannel graphs require extra time to prepare as well as a certain amount of practice in order to be used as effective visual aids. They do, however, provide the novice presenter (adult or child) with the added security of a tangible prop while working before an audience.

FlannelGraphs shows you how to construct a variety of boards and provides you with patterns for a wide range of figures suitable for stories, rhymes, and concept discovery, and for use in many other areas of the curriculum. In addition, many helpful suggestions are given for presenting and using flannel graphs, for involving your students, and for filing and storing materials.

HOW TO MAKE FELT BOARDS

Use any of the following materials for a base: Masonite, plywood, Celotex, bristol board, corrugated cardboard, cork, artist's portfolio, or boards from fabric bolts.

Felt boards, for use with a group, should be approximately two feet by three feet. They can be any shape, but rectangular boards are easier to use and store. A twelve-inch square makes a good lap board for use by either teacher or child. Larger boards can be hinged and folded for easier handling and storage.

A cigar box makes an excellent self-contained flannel graph kit. The outside of the box can be covered or painted and the figures kept in the box. Cover the inside of the lid with felt.

Cover boards with felt or heavy flannel. Yellow, beige, light blue, and black are the most popular colors. In cutting the felt, allow for a two-inch overlap on all sides. Stretch the felt tightly over the board. Secure it to the back side with staples or heavy tape. Do not glue the felt to the board because this weakens the static electricity which is needed to make the figures adhere. The board can also be covered with squares of indoor-outdoor carpet.

For an impromptu board, drape a piece of felt over a painting easel and secure it with several snap clothespins.

Set the finished board on a painting easel, chalk tray, or stand. You can make a satisfactory stand by screwing two large coat hooks into a piece of board twelve inches by three inches by one inch. Various types of easels can also be purchased at art supply stores. For best results, the board should rest at a slight slant.

CONSTRUCTING FIGURES

Select stories that have a few simple figures and repetitive themes. Don't make figures for all the characters or objects. Leave room for the imagination. Detailed backgrounds are hard to work with and are often distracting. However, at times, you may want to add an extra piece of felt for a mountain, sky, or ocean.

Figures can be constructed from felt, interfacing (Pelon), construction paper, or any other material that will adhere to the board. Construction paper figures can be laminated to make them sturdier and to prevent the colors from fading. Figures can be cut from old picture books and from magazines and catalogs. Lightweight paper should be reinforced. Add pieces of felt or sandpaper to the back of paper figures so that they will adhere to the board. Coloring books are a good source for simple patterns. Trace the pattern onto paper and then transfer it to felt. The pattern can be placed directly under Pelon and then traced.

If you wish to enlarge any pattern, use an opaque projector to do so. Simply trace the projected enlargement onto an appropriate material.

TOOLS FOR DECORATING

Felt pens, india ink, colored pencils, crayons, oil paints, and water paints can be used to decorate the figures. After decorating Pelon or felt with crayons or felt pens, place the figures between two sheets of wax paper and press with a warm iron. This will set the colors.

The most attractive and eye-catching patterns are those that are built up. An example of such a pattern is a little boy with boots, mittens, coat, and hat (as on page 69). To make this pattern, first trace and cut out the figure of a boy. Then trace and cut out the boots, mittens, coat, and hat separately. Glue these to the basic figure. You may also cut out the facial features separately. If you use Pelon for the shapes, you can use pieces of felt for decoration.

Super Tacky glue is best for gluing felt. For best results, apply in a dot-to-dot fashion along the edges only. This glue also works well with Pelon.

Always make two sets of figures—one for yourself and one for the children. Children should have the opportunity to work with the figures and to reenact the story or activity. If pieces get lost or torn, you will always have the extra set.

STORAGE

Large manila envelopes make convenient storage places for the cutouts for individual flannel graphs. Fasten a copy of the story to a piece of tagboard or construction paper, and slip it in the envelope. Write the title at the top front, and file the envelope upright in a box. For the children's use, make a paper cutout depicting the contents of the envelope. Paste this to the top front of the envelope. Cover the storage box with colorful, adhesive-backed paper or wallpaper.

Flat boxes that can be stacked are also useful. They should be large enough so the figures can lie flat without being folded.

Self-locking plastic bags are another means for storing figures. Punch a hole in the top of the bag and hang it on a hook or a pegboard. Do not let small children play with plastic bags.

PRESENTATION TECHNIQUES

With practice and adequate preparation, the art of presenting flannel graph stories can soon be mastered. The following checklist will aid you in your presentation.

1. Know your story well. Flannel graph storytelling is a form of oral storytelling, so do not simply read the story. Poems and stories should be memorized.

2. Have your figures arranged in proper sequence so they can be placed on the board quickly and smoothly. Figures can be numbered on the back and placed in order upside down.

3. Place the board where all the children can see it. Do not have it so far from the children that they must strain their eyes or necks in order to see. Place it at a slant and as near the children's eye level as possible. Sit at the same level as the board.

4. After placing a figure on the board, press it firmly with your fingertips.

5. Add figures as they are mentioned. Keep the other figures out of sight, either behind the board or concealed in your lap. Remove all unnecessary figures so the board won't be cluttered and confusing.

6. Keep your eyes on the children, not on the board. Talk to the children, not to the board. This allows you to observe the children's reactions, expressions, and behavior. You will soon be aware of when to speed up, slow down, or repeat information.

7. Encourage children to participate by repeating words, phrases, or actions. Children can add or remove figures when appropriate, if it doesn't detract from the story.

8. If a child is restless or inattentive, try a little trick to recapture interest. Say, for example, "The little girl had brown hair and brown shoes—just like Joannie's" or "Brent, would you please hold the little elf until he is ready to go on the board?"

9. Practice your presentation before doing it for the children.

Concepts and Math Readiness

A Birthday Cake for Me

You will need the following figures: plate, cake, icing, and candles. Use the patterns on page 45 to make them. Cake and icing may be made in several colors so the birthday child can make a choice.

I'm Three

A birthday cake, a birthday cake.   *(Place plate on board.)*
A birthday cake for me.   *(Set cake in plate.)*
How many candles do you see?   *(Add icing to cake.)*
Count them all—one, two, three.   *(Add candles as you count.)*

I'm Four

Candles on my birthday cake.   *(Place plate and cake on board.)*
How many candles will it take?   *(Add icing.)*
Put three here, then add one more.   *(Add candles.)*
For today, you see, I am four.

I'm Five

I ask you now, "What did you bake?"   *(Place plate on board.)*
You answer me, "A birthday cake."   *(Add cake and icing.)*
Now place some candles up on top.   *(Count as you add two candles.)*
When there are five, it's time to stop.   *(Count as you add three more candles.)*
I'll make a wish and blow them out.
For that's what birthdays are all about.

Blue Ribbon Winners

You will need the following figures: white rabbit, yellow sunflower, black lamb, red rooster, pink pig, red tomatoes, four blue ribbons, two red ribbons, father, mother, big brother, big sister, little brother, and little sister. Use the patterns on pages 46 and 47 to make them.

Once upon a time a farmer and his family went to the fair.

(As you mention the family members, place the figures on the board in a vertical row.)

Big brother went to the fair. Big sister went to the fair. Little brother went to the fair. Little sister went to the fair. Father went to the fair. Mother went to the fair.

Big brother took his white rabbit.

(Add rabbit.)

Big sister took her yellow sunflower.

(Add sunflower.)

Little brother took his black lamb.

(Add lamb.)

Little sister took her red rooster.

(Add rooster.)

Father took his pink pig.

(Add pig.)

Mother took her red tomatoes.

(Add tomatoes.)

Big brother's white rabbit won a blue ribbon.

(Place ribbons next to winners as you mention them.)

Big sister's yellow sunflower won a blue ribbon.

Little brother's black lamb won a red ribbon.

Little sister's red rooster won a red ribbon.

Father's pink pig won a blue ribbon.

Mother's red tomatoes won a blue ribbon.

How many blue ribbons did the farmer and his family win?

(Count the ribbons with the children or have a child come to the board and count them.)

How many red ribbons did they win?

(Count.)

How many people are in the family?

(Count.)

Did each person win a ribbon?

(Wait for answer.)

VARIATIONS

Mix up the family members and the objects. Have children match the people to the objects taken to the fair. Older children can also match the ribbons to the objects.

Use the family members to demonstrate ordering—tallest to shortest and shortest to tallest.

Clown Doll

You will need circles, squares, rectangles, and triangles. Use the patterns on page 48 to make them.

First tell the story and make the clown doll for the children. Then retell the story and let the children name the shapes.

Let us make a clown doll. First it needs a nice, round face. We will use a circle.

(Place circle in center of board.)

Next we will add a square for a body.

(Place square under circle.)

Our clown doll needs two arms—one here and another here.

(Add arms.)

These are long rectangles. Two more long rectangles make good legs for our clown doll.

(Add legs.)

Let's give our clown doll a triangle hat.

(Add hat.)

Shall we make a face for our clown?

How many eyes do we need?

(Wait for answer.)

Yes, two.

(Add eyes.)

What else do we need?

(Add nose, mouth, and ears as the children mention them. Patterns for shoes, gloves, pocket, and bow tie are also included.)

VARIATIONS

After children become familiar with the clown doll's shapes and body parts, have them close their eyes or turn around while you remove one shape. Ask children to open their eyes and name the missing part or shape. Return the missing part as it is mentioned. Let children take turns removing parts. With older children, you may be able to remove two pieces at a time.

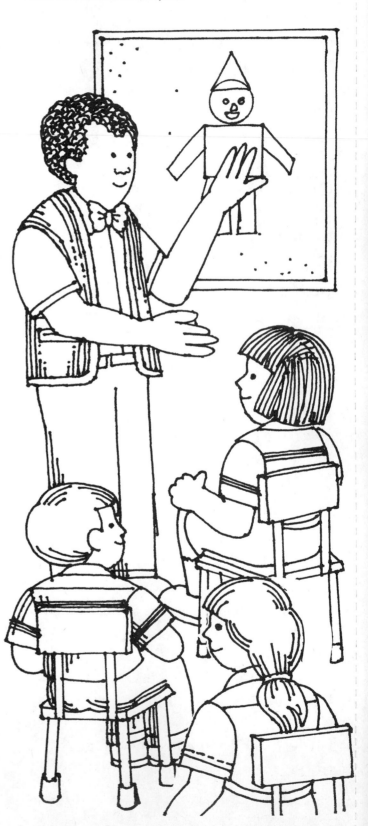

Three of Each

You will need the following figures: three teddy bears, three bow ties, three witches, three hats, three tops, three boys, three caps, and three bunnies. Use the patterns on pages 49 and 50 to make them.

1. Three little teddy bears standing in a row.
   Which one has the bright red bow?

   (Place bears on board. Place a tie on each one.)

2. Three funny witches on their broomsticks sat.
   Which one has the tallest hat?

   (Place witches on board. Place a hat on each one.)

3. Three shiny tops—they're lots of fun.
   Which top is the smallest one?

   (Place tops on board.)

4. Three little boys up from their naps.
   Which two have the same size caps?
   (same color, same shape)

   (Place boys on board. Place a cap on each one.)

5. Three little bunnies without any tears.
   Which one has different ears?

   (Place bunnies on board.)

Discovering Opposites

You will need the following figures: a happy cat face, a sad cat face, a big elephant, a little mouse, a bowl of soup, an ice-cream cone, a black raincoat, a white raincoat, a car, and a feather. Use the patterns on pages 51 and 52 to make them.

1. *(Place happy cat face on board.)*

   This is a happy cat.

   (Place sad cat face next to happy face.)

   This is a sad cat. How can we tell that this is a sad cat?

   (Wait for answer.)

   Show me how a sad cat looks.

   (Pause while children make faces.)

   Let's all look like happy cats.

   (Pause while children make faces.)

   Good! Happy faces make us feel good.

2. *(Place elephant on board.)*

   This is a big elephant.

   (Place mouse next to elephant.)

   This is a little mouse. Can you name something else that is big?

   (Repeat children's answers.)

   Can you name something else that is little?

   (Repeat their answers.)

3. *(Place bowl of soup on board.)*

   This soup is hot.

   (Place ice-cream cone next to soup.)

   This ice cream is cold.

   (Point to the soup.)

   Is it hot or cold?

   (Point to the ice-cream cone.)

   Is it hot or cold?

4. *(Place black raincoat on board.)*

   This raincoat is black.

   (Place white raincoat next to black one.)

   This raincoat is white.

   (Point to black raincoat.)

   Is this raincoat white?

5. *(Place feather on board.)*

   A feather is light.

   (Place car next to feather.)

   A car is heavy.

   (Point to feather.)

   Is this feather light?

VARIATIONS

1. Mix up all the figures. Have children take turns finding the two opposites.

2. Let children choose a figure and ask questions about it. (Is it big? Is it white? Is it heavy?)

3. Have children name qualities of objects in the classroom and name objects with opposite qualities. (The clock is round; the rug is square. The desk is heavy; the paper clip is light.)

4. Make additional figures for the children to practice with.

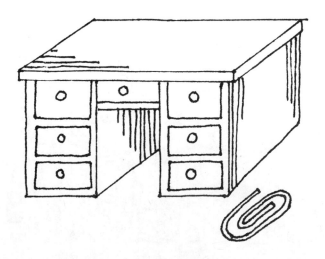

Six Little Snowpeople

You will need six snowpeople and six hats. Use the patterns on page 53 to make them.

Six little snowpeople round and fat.

(*Count the snowpeople as you place them on the board.*)

Each one wore a tall, red hat.

(*Count each hat as you place it on each head.*)

The first red hat blew up in a tree.

(*Remove first hat.*)

The second red hat fell into the sea.

(*Remove second hat.*)

The third red hat got covered with
    snow.

(*Remove third hat.*)

The fourth red hat was eaten by a
    crow.

(*Remove fourth hat.*)

The fifth red hat got stomped by a
    shoe.

(*Remove fifth hat.*)

The sixth red hat tumbled into the
    zoo.

(*Remove sixth hat.*)

Six little snowpeople round and fat,
And not one has a tall, red hat.

(*For older children, repeat the rhyme and, as each hat is removed, ask, "How many hats are left?" If necessary, count with the children.*)

Five Orange Pumpkins

You will need five orange pumpkins (giant, large, medium, small, and tiny) and one small, headless ghost. Use the patterns on page 54 to make them. Draw a jack-o'-lantern face on the reverse side of the tiny pumpkin.

Once there were five orange pumpkins growing in a pumpkin patch.
(Place each one on the board as you mention it.)
There was a giant pumpkin, a large pumpkin, a medium pumpkin, a small pumpkin, and a tiny pumpkin.
A man came by and looked at the five pumpkins. The man picked up the giant pumpkin. "This will be a fine pumpkin to put in my store window," he said.

(Remove giant pumpkin.)

A woman came by and looked at the four pumpkins. The woman picked up the large pumpkin. "This will be a fine pumpkin to set on my doorstep," she said.

(Remove large pumpkin.)

A teacher came by and looked at the three pumpkins. The teacher picked up the medium pumpkin. "This will be a fine pumpkin for my classroom," he said.

(Remove medium pumpkin.)

A baker came by and looked at the two pumpkins. The baker picked up the small pumpkin. "This will be a fine pumpkin for a pie," she said.

(Remove small pumpkin.)

A little boy came by and looked at the tiny pumpkin. The little boy picked up the tiny pumpkin. "This will be a fine pumpkin for my ghost costume," he said. So he painted a face on the pumpkin. Then he put the jack-o'-lantern on top of his head.

(Place ghost under the pumpkin head.)

They both went off to the party, and it was the best Halloween a ghost and a pumpkin ever had.

VARIATIONS

1. Mix up the pumpkins and have children put them in order from largest to smallest and smallest to largest.

2. Ask, "How many pumpkins were in the pumpkin patch?" "Which pumpkin was the first to be picked?" "Which pumpkin was the last to be picked?"

3. Place pumpkins so there is one at the top, one at the bottom, one on the right, one on the left, and one in the center (middle). Have a child come up and identify each position as you name it. (Example: "Show me the pumpkin on the bottom.")

Four Happy Clowns

You will need four clowns and four hats. Use the patterns on page 55 to make them. Each clown's hat should match its collar.

Once there were four happy clowns who worked for the circus.

(Count the clowns as you place them on the board.)

The clowns all wore hats that matched their collars.

(As you place each hat on a clown's head, identify the color. Example: "This clown has a red collar and wears a red hat.")

The four clowns were getting ready to perform their first trick. Suddenly, a strong wind blew their hats off.

(Remove hats and place at random.)

Can you help the clowns find their own hats?

What color hat does the first clown need?

(Have a child replace the hat.)

What color hat does the second clown need?

(Have a child replace the hat.)

What color hat does the third clown need?

(Have a child replace the hat.)

What color hat does the fourth clown need?

(Have a child replace the hat.)

(Turn clowns and hats over and repeat the activity.)

VARIATIONS

Turn clowns and hats over and make matching designs on the other side of each set. Decorate hats and collars with circles (cut circles out with a hole punch and glue them on), hearts, leaves, and flowers. Use a felt pen to make stripes or a plaid design.

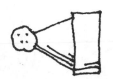

Shamrocks, Pines, and Valentines

You will need the following figures: four shamrocks, five pine trees, and six valentines. Use the patterns on page 56 to make them. Turn one pine tree over and decorate it like a Christmas tree.

Shamrocks

Patty had three green shamrocks.

(Count the shamrocks as you place them on the board.)

Each shamrock had three petals.

(Count the petals.)

One night, a tiny leprechaun came and left another shamrock.

(Add fourth shamrock.)

How many shamrocks does Patty have?

(Wait for answer, then instruct the children to either close their eyes or turn around.)

The next night, the playful leprechaun came again and hid some of Patty's shamrocks.

(Remove three shamrocks.)

Open your eyes. How many shamrocks did the leprechaun hide?

(Wait for answer.)

Yes, three.

(Place the three shamrocks in a group.)

Who has more shamrocks, Patty or the leprechaun?

(Wait for answer.)

Yes, the leprechaun has more. He has three, and Patty has one. How can we share the shamrocks so Patty and the leprechaun will each have the same number of shamrocks?

(Wait for answer.)

Pine Trees

A farmer planted five pine trees.

(Count the trees as you place them on the board.)

While the farmer slept, a little mole came and pulled two trees under the ground into his mole hole.

(Pull the decorated tree plus another one toward the bottom of the board and remove them.)

The next morning the farmer went out to water the trees. How many pine trees did the farmer find?

(Count with the children.)

The little mole didn't like the taste of the trees, so he pushed one back up.

(Place the undecorated tree on the bottom of the board and push it up in line with the others.)

Now how many trees does the farmer have?

(Wait for answer.)

How many trees are missing?

(Wait.)

Where do you think the other tree is?

(Allow children to offer answers. Then place the other tree at the bottom of the board, decorated side down.)

I think the little mole kept it for his Christmas tree.

(Turn the tree over.)

Don't you?

Valentines

Andy has six red valentines.

(Count as you place each one on the board.)

Andy gave three away to his friends.

(Remove three valentines.)

How many does he have left?

(Wait for answer.)

Andy sent one to his grandmother.

(Remove one valentine.)

How many does he have left?

(Wait.)

Andy gave a valentine to me.

(Remove one valentine.)

Now how many valentines does he have?

(Wait.)

Andy's teacher gave him a valentine.

(Add one valentine.)

How many valentines does Andy have?

(Wait.)

The next day, Andy went to school. He found four valentines on his desk.

(Add four valentines.)

Count Andy's valentines to see how many he now has.

(Count with the children.)

Yes, Andy has six valentines. He had a happy Valentine's Day.

Ladybugs, Ladybugs

You will need three to five ladybugs and six to fifteen black spots. Use the patterns on page 57 to make them. Read the rhyme and pause after each question. Have children answer with "The ladybug with ___ spots."

Ladybugs, ladybugs, orange with
    black dots,
Which little ladybug has the most
    spots?

(Place bugs on board.)

Ladybugs, ladybugs, flying off to
    town,
Which one is up and which one is
    down?

(Place two bugs on the board, one higher than the other.)

Ladybugs, ladybugs, crawling up a
    tree,
Which one is stopped right next to
    me?

(Place bugs with heads facing up and with one bug close to you.)

Ladybugs, ladybugs, marching off to
    play,
Which one is turned the other way?

(Place bugs in a line, with one bug facing in the opposite direction.)

Little Brown Snail

You will need the following figures: a brown snail, a whale, a pail, a dog, a nail, some mail, and a sailboat. Use the patterns on page 58. Instead of using the pattern for the nail, you could glue a real nail to a circle of felt. For the mail, glue a few stamped envelopes on a circle of felt. As you mention each item in the poem, place it on the board. Then move the snail to the appropriate position.

Little brown snail,   *(Place snail on board.)*
Whose name was Gail,
Left her trail,
Over a whale,
Upon a pail,
Around a tail,
Across a nail,
Under the mail,
Behind a sail,
And that's the tale
Of Gail the snail.

VARIATIONS

1. Place the snail in different positions on the board. Ask the children, "Is Gail on the whale or under the whale?"

2. Have children take turns placing the snail and then identifying the position.

3. Give directions such as, "Please put Gail on top of the whale."

4. Expand the activity by adding additional concepts—*below, next to, between, near,* and *through.*

5. Add other words that rhyme with *snail.* There are many words that do, and older children will enjoy thinking of them.

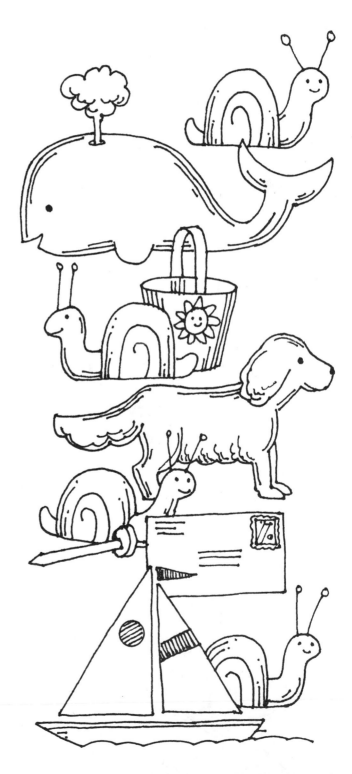

Stop and Go Light

You will need the following figures: stoplight frame, red circle, yellow circle, green circle, eyes, ears, standing feet, and walking feet. Use the patterns on page 59 to make them.

Here is a stoplight.   *(Place frame on board.)*
When the light is red,   *(Add red circle at top.)*
No, no. You must not go.
When the light is yellow,   *(Add yellow circle.)*
Wait, wait. Even if you're late.
When the light is green,   *(Add green circle.)*
Don't talk! Just walk.

When you don't see a stoplight,
Stop!   *(Place standing feet on board.)*
Look!   *(Place eyes on board.)*
Listen!   *(Place ears on board.)*
Stop, look, and listen for cars
Before you cross the street,
Then use your feet.   *(Place walking feet on board.)*

Wonders of Science

Grandpa's Magic Seed

You will need the following figures: real sunflower seed glued to a small piece of felt, roots, stems (two stem sections), small and large leaves, sunflower, and seed pod. Use the patterns on page 60, as needed. (Instead of using the pattern for the roots, you could glue pieces of string or yarn to a small piece of felt.)

One day Grandpa gave Amos a seed.
(Place seed in the center of board.)

"Take it home," Grandpa said. "Plant it in your garden where the sun shines brightly. Water it every day. And one day it will give you a hundred seeds."

"What kind of a seed is it?" asked Amos.

"You will see," answered Grandpa.

Amos called it his magic seed. He planted it in a sunny spot and watered it every day, just as Grandpa said.
(Move seed near the bottom of board.)

Amos couldn't see them, but underneath the ground, tiny roots were growing.
(Place roots under seed.)

Then one day, Amos saw a tiny green sprout. "It's growing!" he shouted.

Every day Amos watered his plant. The stem grew taller and taller.
(Add one stem.)

Soon two green heart-shaped leaves appeared.
(Add two small leaves, one on each side of stem.)

Amos kept watering his plant. It kept growing.
(Add second stem section, raise small leaves, and add large leaves to bottom stem.)

It grew taller than Amos.

Soon a flower with yellow petals and a brown center bloomed at the top of Amos's plant.
(Add sunflower.)

In the morning, the flower turned toward the sun.
(Turn flower toward the east.)

The flower followed the sun as it moved across the sky. In the evening, it was facing the other way.
(Move flower slowly, so it turns toward the west.)

"Now I have a magic flower," said Amos.

For many months, Amos's plant stood tall and beautiful in his garden. And then the flower drooped and the petals started to fall.
(Bend top stem and flower.)

Amos was feeling sad when Grandpa came to visit. "My magic seed plant has died," he said.

"Let's take a look," said Grandpa.
(Replace sunflower with seed pod.)

"See all the seeds. You grew a sunflower and now it has gone to seed. You can roast the seeds and eat them. Birds like them, too."

"There are hundreds of seeds," laughed Amos. "I will roast some to eat, give some to the birds, and save one. Next year I will plant my seed and grow another sunflower. It really was a magic seed, wasn't it, Grandpa?"

The Mushroom in the Meadow

You will need the following figures: mushroom, spotted ladybug, red ant, black beetle, green grasshopper, yellow butterfly, and white rabbit. Use the patterns on pages 61 and 62 to make them.

In the middle of a grassy meadow grew a giant mushroom.

(Place mushroom in center of board.)

Spotted ladybug flew into the meadow.

(Fly ladybug onto board.)

Spotted ladybug walked around the mushroom.

(Walk ladybug around the mushroom and place it on board near mushroom.)

Red ant crawled into the meadow.

(Crawl ant onto board.)

Red ant walked around the mushroom.

(Walk ant around the mushroom and place it on board near ladybug.)

Black beetle tumbled into the meadow.

(Tumble beetle onto board.)

Black beetle walked around the mushroom.

(Walk beetle around the mushroom and place it on board near ant.)

Green grasshopper hopped into the meadow.

(Hop grasshopper onto board.)

Green grasshopper walked around the mushroom.

(Walk grasshopper around the mushroom and place it on board near beetle.)

Yellow butterfly fluttered into the meadow.

(Flutter butterfly onto board.)

Yellow butterfly walked around the mushroom.

(Walk butterfly around the mushroom and place it on board near grasshopper.)

Around and around and around they went.

(Move insects around the mushroom.)

White rabbit jumped into the meadow.

(Jump rabbit onto board and move it to the mushroom.)

White rabbit ate the mushroom.

(Cover mushroom with your hand and remove it.)

White rabbit jumped away.

(Jump rabbit off board.)

Now spotted ladybug couldn't walk around the mushroom, so spotted ladybug flew away.

(Remove ladybug.)

Now red ant couldn't walk around the mushroom, so red ant crawled away.

(Remove ant.)

Now black beetle couldn't walk around the mushroom, so black beetle tumbled away.

(Remove beetle.)

Now green grasshopper couldn't walk around the mushroom, so green grasshopper hopped away.

(Remove grasshopper.)

Now yellow butterfly couldn't walk around the mushroom, so yellow butterfly flew away.

(Remove butterfly.)

Olie and the Cloud

You will need the following figures: boy, gray squirrel, redheaded woodpecker, owl, and a reversible cloud. Use the patterns on page 63 to make them. On the back of the cloud, draw tears to represent rain.

Olie was a little boy who lived on a farm.

(Place boy on board.)

It was a beautiful farm and everything was growing well. The grass was green, the garden was growing, and the flowers were blooming. Then for a long, long time there was not any rain. Everything was turning brown and starting to die. Olie decided that if he could talk to the clouds, maybe they would send him some rain. So early one morning, he started out to climb the biggest tree on the farm to see if he could reach the clouds.

He started up the tree.

(Move Olie to the bottom of board.)

He met a gray, fuzzy squirrel.

(Add squirrel.)

"Chee-chee," said the squirrel. "You can't come up here unless you pay me four nuts."

"I have no nuts," said Olie, "but I have four cents."

"Chee-chee," said the squirrel. "No money, just nuts."

"But I have to get to the top of this tree to get water," said Olie. "I do have a peanut butter sandwich in my pocket. Will you take that?"

"Well, let me try it," said the squirrel. "Chee-chee, umm, that does taste pretty good. Okay, you may pass."

(Remove squirrel.)

Olie climbed on.

(Move Olie up the board.)

Soon he met an owl.

(Add owl.)

The owl was half asleep. "Hoot-hoot," he said, "who goes there?"

"It is me, Olie," he said.

"What are you doing in my tree," asked the owl, "waking me up like this?"

"Oh, I'm sorry," said Olie, "but I must get to the top of this tree for I need water."

"Well, it will cost you two pineapples," said the owl.

"I don't have two pineapples," said Olie, "but I do have a big, red apple."

"Okay, give it to me," said the owl, "and you may pass."
(Remove owl.)

Olie kept climbing up the tree.
(Move Olie up the board.)

Soon he met a redheaded woodpecker.
(Add woodpecker.)

"Rat-a-tat-tat," went the woodpecker. "Rat-a-tat-tat, what are you doing here?"

"I must get to the top of this tree to get some water," said Olie. The woodpecker was so busy that he didn't pay any attention and let Olie pass.
(Remove woodpecker.)

Olie climbed and climbed.
(Move Olie up the board.)

Soon he was at the top. There he saw Mr. Cloud.
(Add cloud.)

"Please, Mr. Cloud," he said, "may I have some water?"

"No," said Mr. Cloud, "I am saving my water for a rainy day."

"Oh, but I must have water," said Olie. "I live on a farm and all the little plants, the corn, the grass, and the flowers will die—even the animals might die—if we don't get some water."

This made Mr. Cloud very sad and all at once the tears rolled down his face. He started to cry.
(Turn cloud over.)

He cried and cried until the water fell down all over the farm. Now there was plenty of water.

Olie thanked Mr. Cloud.
(Remove cloud.)

He climbed down the tree.
(Move Olie to bottom of board.)

He went back to his happy little farm.
(Slowly move Olie off the board.)

Polly's Not a Fish

You will need the following figures: eggs, polliwog, set of front legs, set of back legs, green frog, and lily pad. Use the patterns on page 64 to make them. You will also need an oval piece of blue felt for the pond.

In this pond near the woods lived many little fish.
(Place pond on board.)
Polly lived there, too. Polly didn't know it but she had hatched from a tiny egg.
(Place eggs and polliwog on side of pond.)
Polly swam and swam.
(Remove eggs.)
She was happy there.

Soon Polly began to grow fatter. Then she grew two long, strong back legs.
(Add back legs.)

"Look at me," she called to the fish. But the fish just went on swimming. Polly swam too.

In a few days, she grew two short front legs and her tail started to disappear.
(Add front legs.)
But she didn't mind, for with her new legs she could swim very fast. Polly was swimming through the water and pushing with her back legs. Polly was jumping! She jumped right out of the water.
(Remove polliwog.)
She landed on a lily pad.
(Place lily pad on pond and set frog on it.)
Polly jumped in and out of the water. She spent the day swimming and splashing and diving.
(Move frog about and then back to lily pad.)

Polly hopped back onto the lily pad to rest. She looked down in the water and saw herself. And Polly knew that she had never been a fish. When she hatched from the egg, she was a polliwog. After she lost her tail and grew legs, she was a frog—a beautiful, green frog. Polly was happy to be a frog. She jumped from the lily pad and over to the bank. Then off she went to find a place to lay her eggs.
(Jump frog to edge of pond and then off the board. Remove lily pad. Remove pond.)

Seven Beautiful Colors

You will need seven curved bands. See patterns on page 65 for correct curves and colors. Since it is difficult to find the exact colors of felt, it is best to use Pelon and color the bands with felt pens.

Once there was a great artist who painted with many beautiful colors. Sometimes, though, she was rather messy and dropped the paint on the floor. One day she began to paint a large picture. She dipped her brush into the red paint and brushed it onto her canvas. Some of the paint spilled to the floor and made a curved streak just like this.

(Place red band near top of board.)

The artist kept on painting. She dipped her brush into the orange paint and brushed it onto her canvas. Some of the orange paint spilled to the floor and made a curved orange streak right here.

(Place orange band under red band.)

The artist kept on painting. She dipped her brush into the yellow paint and brushed it onto her canvas. Some of the yellow paint spilled to the floor and made a curved yellow streak right here.

(Place yellow band under orange band.)

The artist kept on painting. She dipped her brush into the green paint and brushed it onto her canvas. Some of the green paint spilled to the floor and made a curved green streak right here.

(Place green band under yellow band.)

The artist kept on painting. She dipped her brush into the blue paint and brushed it onto her canvas. Some of the blue paint spilled to the floor and made a curved blue streak right here.

(Place blue band under green band.)

The artist kept on painting. She dipped her brush into the indigo paint and brushed it onto her canvas. Some of the indigo paint spilled to the floor and made a curved indigo streak right here.

(Place indigo band under blue band.)

The artist kept on painting. She dipped her brush into the violet paint and brushed it onto her canvas. Some of the violet paint fell to the floor and made a curved violet streak right here.

(Place violet band under indigo band.)

That was her last color of paint. The artist looked down at the floor. What did she see? Yes, she saw a rainbow.

A rainbow always has seven colors even though we can't always see them clearly. Let's count the colors.

(Count with the children.)

The colors of the rainbow are always the same and they are always in this order.

(Point to the colors, from top to bottom, and have children name the colors. You may need to explain that indigo is a blue-violet color, and that violet is like purple.)

Let's mix up the rainbow and put it back together.

(Remove bands, then place them on the board at random. Have children take turns putting the rainbow puzzle together while naming the colors.)

A Special Tree

You will need the following figures: basic tree, three treetops, blossoms, apples, and leaves. Use the patterns on page 66 to make them. Glue blossoms to the first treetop, apples to the second, and leaves to the third.

Once there was a tree growing in the garden.

(Place basic tree on board.)

It had no leaves or fruit because it was wintertime. All through the winter, the tree rested, for it would soon have much work to do. The snow fell and the winds blew.

Spring came. The warm sun and the gentle rains woke the tree. Tiny buds began to appear. They turned into little flowers and soon the tree was covered with flowers.

(Add treetop with blossoms.)

Summer came. At the bottom of each flower was a tiny green ball. Soon the flowers fell off and fluttered to the ground. The warm sun and plenty of water helped the tiny green balls grow bigger and bigger. By the end of summer, the tree was covered with red apples.

(Add treetop with apples, covering the treetop with blossoms.)

The apples grew and grew.

Fall came. The boys and girls came and picked all the apples. Only the leaves were left on the tree.

(Add treetop with leaves, covering treetop with apples.)

The leaves began to turn orange, yellow, and gold.

Winter came. The leaves fell off the tree.

(Remove all extra treetops.)

And the tree rested again.

Stories to Tell

The Happy Fruit Tree

You will need the following figures: a yellow banana, a green pear, an orange-colored orange, a red apple, a yellow lemon, a bunch of purple grapes, and a tree with bare branches. Use the patterns on page 67 to make the fruits. Use the pattern for the basic tree on page 66.

At the time of year when the fruit was ripe and ready to be picked, a strange thing happened.

The fruit pickers came through the banana plantations and picked the bananas. They put them in boxes and shipped them off to market. As they chopped off the big stalks of bananas, one small yellow one was left hanging on the tree.

(Place banana near top of board.)

She was sad and lonely, so she decided to go and look for her banana friends.

(Move banana down.)

The banana walked down the long rows of trees. She soon came to an orchard. Hearing a sad sound, she looked up. Hanging on the tree, nearly hidden by a leaf, was a green pear.

(Place pear near top of board.)

"Why are you so sad?" asked the banana.

"When the fruit pickers came, they could not see me because of the leaf, so I was left," answered the pear.

"Come with me," said the banana. "I am going to look for my friends."

The green pear joined the yellow banana.

(Place pear behind banana.)

Together they walked through the orchard. Soon they came upon an orange-colored orange lying in the dirt at the bottom of a tree.

(Place orange in front of banana near bottom of board.)

She, too, looked sad.

"What is the matter?" asked the banana.

"When the orange pickers came, they piled all the oranges into a box," said the orange. "But I rolled off the top, and they left me on the ground."

"Come with us," said the pear. "We are going to look for our friends."

The orange-colored orange joined the green pear and the yellow banana.

(Place orange behind pear.)

They walked through the orchard. High on a tree was one red apple.

(Place apple near top of board.)

"Why are you all alone?" asked the banana.

"I have a small wormhole," answered the apple. "So the pickers left me hanging on the tree."

"Come with us," said the orange. "We are going to look for our friends."

The red apple joined the orange-colored

orange, the green pear, and the yellow banana.

(Place apple behind orange.)

Down through the rows of trees they walked. On a low branch, they saw a yellow lemon.

(Place lemon above center of board.)

"Why are you all alone?" asked the banana.

"The pickers thought I looked too sour, so they left me on the tree."

"Come with us. We are going to look for our friends," said the apple.

The yellow lemon joined the red apple, the orange-colored orange, the green pear, and the yellow banana.

(Place lemon behind apple.)

Soon they left the orchard and entered a vineyard where rows of grapevines grew. On a knotted and twisted vine hung a bunch of purple grapes.

(Place grapes on board.)

"Why are you still on the vine?" asked the banana.

"The pickers did not think that we were purple enough to pick," replied the grapes.

"Come with us," said the lemon. "We are going to look for our friends."

The purple grapes joined the yellow lemon, the red apple, the orange-colored orange, the green pear, and the yellow banana.

(Place grapes behind lemon.)

Together they left the vineyard and walked down the dusty road. Suddenly they came upon an old brown tree without any leaves.

(Place tree in front of banana.)

"Why are you so sad, Mrs. Fruit Tree?" asked the banana.

"All my fruit has been picked," answered the tree. "And the wind has blown off all my leaves. I am sad and lonely."

The friendly group of fruits decided to do something to help the tree. They came up with an idea. Each found a branch where she would be comfortable.

(Place fruit on branches.)

They settled down and spent the night in the tree. This made the tree very happy. The fruits liked it there. They decided to stay and make the tree their new home.

If you should ever come upon a very happy tree, look closely. If you see a yellow banana, a green pear, an orange-colored orange, a red apple, a yellow lemon, and a bunch of purple grapes, it will surely be the Happy Fruit Tree.

Can You Find My Breakfast?

You will need the following figures: a cat, a bowl of milk, a rabbit, a carrot, a cow, a pile of hay, a pig, a cob of corn, a dog, and a bone. Use the patterns on page 68 to make them.

Carlos and Maria lived on a farm. Their job was to feed the animals their breakfasts. Early one morning, Carlos and Maria went to the barn. It was still a little dark, and Carlos and Maria were still a little sleepy.

(As you name each animal, place it on the board. As you name each food, place it next to the animal.)

They gave the cat a carrot.

They gave the rabbit a cob of corn.

They gave the cow a bowl of milk.

They gave the pig a bone.

They gave the dog a pile of hay.

And then Carlos and Maria went off to school.

But the cat didn't eat the carrot. The rabbit didn't eat the corn. The cow didn't drink the milk. The pig didn't eat the bone. The dog didn't eat the hay.

When Carlos and Maria returned from school, they ran to the barn. They laughed when they saw what they had done. Can you help Carlos and Maria feed each animal the right breakfast?

(Remove foods and place them at random across top of board. As children give correct answers, place the food next to the animal.)

What does the cat like?

What does the rabbit like?

What does the cow like?

What does the pig like?

What does the dog like?

Finally, the animals ate their breakfasts.

(Remove foods; then remove the animals.)

The Rollaway Snowperson

You will need the following figures: a boy, boots, mittens, hat, coat, four snowballs, a black hat larger than the boy's, a carrot, five black circles, a banana, a red scarf, and a snowperson. Use the patterns on page 69 to make them.

Once upon a time, a little boy went out to play.
(Place boy on board.)
He put on his red boots, his warm coat and hat, and his red mittens.
(Add the items as you name them.)
He climbed to the top of the hill where the snow was deep.
(Move boy to top of board.)

The little boy started rolling a very small snowball.
(Place small snowball in front of boy.)
Then the snowball started rolling down the hill. As it rolled, it grew bigger and bigger and bigger.
(Slowly move snowball and boy down the board as you tell the rest of the story, covering each snowball with a larger one as necessary.)

As the snowball rolled along, it ran into a man with a tall black hat.
(Place hat in front of snowball.)
The snowball gathered up the hat.
(Cover hat with the two smallest snowballs.)

It ran into a rabbit eating a carrot.
(Place carrot in front of snowballs.)
And it gathered up the carrot.
(Place snowballs over carrot.)

It rolled into a clown juggling five black balls.
(Place black balls in front of snowballs.)
And it gathered up the five balls.
(Place snowballs over balls.)

It ran into a monkey eating a banana.
(Place banana in front of snowballs.)
And it gathered up the banana.
(Place snowballs over banana.)

It ran into a little girl wearing a bright red scarf.
(Place scarf in front of snowballs.)
And it gathered up the scarf.
(Place snowballs over scarf.)

At the bottom of the hill, the snowball hit a bump.
(Separate items as you name them.)
Now there were four snowballs, a hat, a scarf, five balls, a carrot, and a banana. Then a strange thing happened.
(Remove all objects.)
All but the smallest snowball came together and became the most beautiful snowperson that the little boy had ever seen.
(Place snowperson on board near boy.)

A Ghost Called Matt

You will need the following figures: five short, fat ghosts (blue, yellow, black, orange, and brown); a yellow moon; an orange jack-o'-lantern; a witch in a black dress; and a brown owl. Use the patterns on page 70 to make them.

Once there was a little blue ghost.
(Place blue ghost on board.)
His name was Matthew but everyone called him Matt. Matt was short and fat, and he lived with the other ghosts in the Old Ghost Hotel.

One dark Halloween night, Matt decided that he didn't like being a blue ghost, so he set out to find himself a new color.

Matt looked up and saw the full yellow moon.
(Add moon.)
"There's the color for me," he thought. And he said,

> I'm a ghost called Matt,
> I'm short and fat,
> And I can change my color
> Just like that.

(Clap your hands and substitute the yellow ghost. Encourage children to participate by clapping hands and repeating chant.)

Matt flew back to the Old Ghost Hotel to show the other ghosts his new color.
(Remove moon.)
They looked at Matt and said,

> Ho, ho, ho.
> Hee, hee, hee.
> You're the funniest-looking ghost
> We ever did see.

Matt flew out the window and went looking for a new color. He saw a witch flying through the sky. She was wearing a black dress.
(Add witch.)
"There's the color for me," he thought. And then he said,

> I'm a ghost called Matt,
> I'm short and fat,
> And I can change my color
> Just like that.

(Clap your hands and substitute the black ghost.)

Matt flew back to the Old Ghost Hotel to show the other ghosts his new color.
(Remove witch.)
They looked at Matt and said,

> Ho, ho, ho.
> Hee, hee, hee.
> You're the funniest-looking ghost
> We ever did see.

Matt flew out the window and went looking for a new color. He saw an orange jack-o'-lantern sitting on the fence.
(Add jack-o'-lantern.)
"That's the color for me," he thought. And then he said,

> I'm a ghost called Matt,
> I'm short and fat,
> And I can change my color
> Just like that.

(Clap your hands and substitute the orange ghost.)

Matt flew back to the Old Ghost Hotel to show the other ghosts his new color.
(Remove jack-o'-lantern.)
They looked at Matt and said,

> Ho, ho, ho.
> Hee, hee, hee.
> You're the funniest-looking ghost
> We ever did see.

Matt flew out the window and went looking for a new color. He saw a brown owl sitting in a tree.
(Add owl.)
"That's the color for me," he thought. And then he said,

> I'm a ghost called Matt,
> I'm short and fat,
> And I can change my color
> Just like that.

(Clap your hands and substitute the brown ghost.)

Matt flew off to the Old Ghost Hotel to show the other ghosts his new color.
(Remove owl.)
They looked at him and said,

> Ho, ho, ho.
> Hee, hee, hee.
> You're the funniest-looking ghost
> We ever did see.

Matt flew out the window and went looking for a new color. He flew around and around.

(Place ghosts across top of board as you mention each color.)
"I don't want to be a yellow ghost. I don't want to be a black ghost. I don't want to be an orange ghost. I don't want to be a brown ghost. I just want to be me—I want to be a blue ghost." And so he said,

> I'm a ghost called Matt,
> I'm short and fat,
> And I can change my color
> Just like that.

(Clap your hands and remove the yellow, black, orange, and brown ghosts. Place Matt on board.)

Matt flew back to the Old Ghost Hotel. This time the other ghosts didn't laugh. "Come on," they called, "let's go ghosting." Now Matt was happy to be a blue ghost and away he went.

The Witch Who Couldn't Fly

You will need the following figures: Wilma Witch, Gabby Ghost, Jackie Lantern, Kati Kat, Ollie Owl, a group of witches, and a red schoolhouse. Use the patterns on page 71 to make them.

Wilma was a little witch who was trying to learn to fly.

(Place Wilma on board.)

She had been trying all year in hopes that this year she could go Halloween-ing with all the other witches who lived in Witchville. Every day she tried and tried. But Wilma could not fly.

"In just one week it will be Halloween," she said. "I must learn to fly."

It was Sunday.

(Change the days to start the story one week before Halloween.)

All the witches in Witchville came to help Wilma learn to fly.

(Place witches near the top of the board, on the left side.)

They tried and tried to help their friend, but Wilma still couldn't fly.

On Monday, they sent her to flying school.

(Place red schoolhouse next to the witches.)

The teachers tried and tried to help her, but Wilma still couldn't fly.

On Tuesday, Gabby Ghost came to help Wilma learn to fly.

(Place Gabby next to the schoolhouse.)

He tried and tried to help his friend, but Wilma still couldn't fly.

On Wednesday, Jackie Lantern came to help Wilma learn to fly.

(Place Jackie next to Gabby.)

She tried and tried to help her friend, but Wilma still couldn't fly.

On Thursday, Kati Kat came to help Wilma learn to fly.

(Place Kati next to Jackie.)

She tried and tried to help her friend, but Wilma still couldn't fly.

On Friday, Ollie Owl came to help Wilma learn to fly.

(Place Ollie next to Kati.)

He tried and tried to help his friend, but Wilma still couldn't fly.

It was Saturday, Halloween. The big night had finally arrived. Wilma had not learned to fly on Sunday.

(Point out corresponding characters as you mention days of the week.)

She had not learned to fly on Monday. She had not learned to fly on Tuesday. She had not learned to fly on Wednesday. She had not learned to fly on Thursday. She had not learned to fly on Friday.

Wilma felt sad as she watched the other witches dusting and polishing their broomsticks. She sat in the corner on her own little broom and watched her friends, one by one, fly away.

(Remove witches.)

"Oh, I wish I could fly, too." she said to herself.

Gabby Ghost, Jackie Lantern, Kati Kat, and Ollie Owl crept up behind Wilma Witch.

(Move Wilma to the right of board and place other figures in a row behind her.)

They all yelled, "Boo!"

Zoom! Wilma Witch took off on her broom.

(Move as directed.)

Up, up, up she went. Higher and higher she flew. Around and around, up and down, and back and forth. Wilma Witch laughed and laughed. "I'm flying! I'm flying!" she yelled. And for all we know, Wilma Witch may still be up there flying around and around.

(Remove Wilma.)

Mixed-Up Holidays

You will need the following figures: a basket and three colored eggs; white lace and three red hearts; a star, a bell, and a stocking; ghost, witch, and jack-o'-lantern cookies; pumpkin pie, sweet potatoes, and roast turkey. Use the patterns on page 72 to make them. You will also need some extra red paper backed with flannel.

Aunt Fanny lived all alone in a big house in the country. Her nieces and nephews were coming to spend the holiday. She wasn't really sure which holiday it was, for sometimes Aunt Fanny got things mixed up.

"I know which holiday it is," she said. Aunt Fanny set out a little basket and dyed three pretty eggs.
(Place basket and eggs on board.)
Which holiday is she getting ready for?
(Wait for answer.)
Yes, Easter.

Aunt Fanny heard a small whisper, "No, no, tomorrow is not Easter."
(Remove items.)

"Now I know which holiday it is," she said. Aunt Fanny set out some red paper and some white lace. She took her scissors and cut out three red hearts.
(Place red paper, lace, and hearts on board.)
Which holiday is she getting ready for?
(Wait for answer.)
Yes, Valentine's Day.

Aunt Fanny heard a small whisper, "No, no, tomorrow is not Valentine's Day."
(Remove items.)

"Now I know which holiday it is," she said. Aunt Fanny got out a star and a bell and started decorating her house. She hung up her stocking.
(Place star, bell, and stocking on board.)
Which holiday is she getting ready for?
(Wait for answer.)
Yes, Christmas.

Aunt Fanny heard a small whisper, "No, no, tomorrow is not Christmas."
(Remove items.)

"Now I know which holiday it is," she said. Aunt Fanny made some cookies. She made one like this.
(Add ghost.)
She made one like this.
(Add witch.)
And she made one like this.
(Add jack-o'-lantern.)

Which holiday is she getting ready for?
(Wait for answer.)

Yes, Halloween.

Aunt Fanny heard a small whisper, "No, no, tomorrow is not Halloween."
(Remove items.)

"Now I know which holiday it is," she said. Aunt Fanny baked a pumpkin pie, cooked the sweet potatoes, and started to roast the turkey.
(Place pie, potatoes, and turkey on board.)

Aunt Fanny's not mixed up anymore. She knows which holiday it is. Do you?
(Wait for answer.)

Yes, Thanksgiving. Now Aunt Fanny is ready for her nieces and nephews.

(You can also use this story for Halloween, Easter, Christmas, or Valentine's Day by rearranging the order of the holidays.)

Who's in the Forest?

You will need the following figures: one large brown triangle, two small brown triangles, two small black rectangles, two white circles, two small black circles, and one red circle. Cover the red circle with glue and sprinkle it with glitter. Use the patterns on page 73 to make them.

Late one Christmas Eve, Anita and Roberto were picking up pinecones near the edge of the forest.

"It's getting dark," said Roberto. "We should start home."

"Just a few more pinecones," said Anita, "and our basket will be full."

The children moved farther into the forest.

"Oh, here are some giant pinecones," called Roberto. "Help me gather some of these."

Anita and Roberto started picking up the giant pinecones. They looked up and saw something moving between the pine branches. Quietly they moved back into the shadows. Anita and Roberto sat very still.

(Whisper.)
They watched and watched and waited and waited.

Through the green branches, there appeared a large brown triangle.
(Place triangle with point downward.)

Anita and Roberto sat very still.

(Whisper.)
They watched and watched and waited and waited.

Through the green branches, there appeared two small brown triangles.
(Place small brown triangles on side of board.)
One came to rest right here.
(Place it at the top right corner of the large triangle, point up.)
And the other came to rest right here.
(Place it on the top left corner of the triangle, point up.)

Anita and Roberto sat very still.

(Whisper.)
They watched and watched and waited and waited.

Through the green branches, there appeared two black rectangles. They came to rest between the two small brown triangles that sat on the large brown triangle.
(Place rectangles in position.)

Anita and Roberto sat very still.

(Whisper.)
They watched and watched and waited and waited.

Through the green branches, there appeared two white circles.
(Place circles on side of board.)
Inside each circle was a small black circle.
(Place black circles.)
The circles came to rest right here.
(Place them on brown triangle for eyes.)

Anita and Roberto sat very still.

(Whisper.)

They watched and watched and waited and waited.

Through the green branches, there appeared a shiny red circle.

(Place red circle on side of board.)

It came to rest right here.

(Place red circle for nose.)

It lit up the whole forest. Anita and Roberto jumped up from their hiding place, grabbed their basket of pinecones, and ran all the way home. They never did find out what was coming through the green branches on that dark Christmas Eve. Do you know what it was?

(Wait for answer.)

Yes, it was a red-nosed reindeer.

VARIATION

Have the children whisper the refrain, "They watched and watched and waited and waited."

The Easter People

You will need the following figures: brown bunny, yellow duck (can be sprinkled with glitter), yellow chick, painted egg with gold egg glued to back, pink jelly bean, Easter Rabbit, and basket with a pocket (double thickness, open at top). Use the patterns on page 74 to make them. Place all figures, except Easter Rabbit, in pocket of basket. Set basket at top center of board.

The Easter people
Jumped out one night,
When the Easter Rabbit
Was out of sight.

(Remove bunny from basket and place on board.)

The chocolate bunny
Wiggled his nose
And danced around
On his candy toes.

(Remove duck from basket and place on board.)

The sugary duck
Started to quack
And shook the feathers
Right off her back.

(Remove chick from basket and place on board.)

The marshmallow chick
Went, "Cheep, cheep, cheep,"
And hoped the rabbit
Would stay asleep.

(Remove egg from basket and place on board.)

Pretty, painted egg
Rolled and rolled.
His paint rubbed off
And now he is gold.

(Turn egg over.)

(Remove jelly bean from basket and place on board.)

The pink jelly bean
Bounced up and down.
And then she twisted,
And turned around.

They were so happy
To be out to play,
They almost forgot
It was Easter Day.

And then one by one,
Back in they popped.

(Return figures to basket.)

The rabbit came by,

(Place rabbit near basket.)

Away he hopped.

(Remove rabbit with basket.)

No Eggs for Easter

You will need the following figures: Easter Rabbit; Mrs. Hen, Mrs. Duck, and Mrs. Turkey, each sitting on a nest; a cluster each of brown, white, and speckled eggs; three circles to glue the eggs on; a chick, a duckling, and a baby turkey. Use the patterns on pages 75 and 76 to make them. On the back of the circle with white eggs, glue the chick; on the back of the circle with brown eggs, glue the duckling; on the back of the circle with speckled eggs, glue the baby turkey.

Once there was an Easter Rabbit who liked to sleep.

(Place rabbit on board.)

He slept all winter.

(Put rabbit in reclining position.)

When spring came, he was still sleeping.

Late one afternoon, Easter Rabbit woke up.

(Stand rabbit up.)

He yawned and he yawned and he stretched and he stretched. He rubbed his eyes and yawned again. Easter Rabbit checked the calendar and saw that tomorrow was Easter Sunday.

"Oh, whatever will I do?" he wondered. "Tomorrow is Easter and I don't have my Easter eggs ready." He checked around his rabbit house. But there were no eggs there.

He went to the rabbit egg store. "No eggs here," said the store rabbit. "We are all sold out."

He called his rabbit friends. "Sorry," they said. "We have no eggs left."

Easter Rabbit was worried. "I must find some eggs," he said. "It's getting late."

Easter Rabbit hurried out to the old farm.

(Hop rabbit across board.)

Hop, hop, hop he went. He found Mrs. Hen sitting on a nest of eggs.

(Place hen in front of rabbit.)

"Please, Mrs. Hen," he said, "may I have some of your eggs to paint for the children?"

"Why, yes," said Mrs. Hen. "Take them all."

Easter Rabbit thanked Mrs. Hen and gathered all of her white eggs.

(Have rabbit gather eggs. Remove hen.)

"This is not nearly enough," he thought.

Then he saw Mrs. Duck sitting on a nest of eggs.

(Place duck in front of rabbit.)

"Please, Mrs. Duck," he said. "May I have some of your eggs to paint for the children?"

"Why, yes," said Mrs. Duck. "Take them all."

Easter Rabbit thanked Mrs. Duck and gathered all of her brown eggs.

(Have rabbit gather eggs. Remove duck.)

"This is not nearly enough," he thought.

Then he saw Mrs. Turkey sitting on a nest of eggs.

(Place turkey in front of rabbit.)

"Please, Mrs. Turkey," he said. "May I have some of your eggs to paint for the children?"

"Why, yes," said Mrs. Turkey. "Take them all."

Easter Rabbit thanked Mrs. Turkey and gathered all of her speckled eggs.

(Have rabbit gather eggs. Remove turkey.)

Then he started home. Hop, hop, hop he went.

When Easter Rabbit got home, he was so sleepy. He set the eggs on the floor and yawned and yawned.

"I must hurry and paint these eggs," he said. "I will paint some green, some purple, and some orange. But first I will take a little nap." Easter Rabbit leaned back in his chair.

(Tilt rabbit back.)

Soon he fell asleep.

While he slept, the eggs began to shake and jiggle.

(Move egg clusters about.)

Crack, crack, crack. Easter Rabbit slept on.

Crack, crack, crack. Mrs. Hen's eggs cracked open and out came some little yellow chicks.

(Turn cluster over.)

Easter Rabbit slept on.

Crack, crack, crack. Mrs. Duck's eggs cracked open and out came some fuzzy, white ducklings.

(Turn cluster over.)

Still Easter Rabbit slept on.

Crack, crack, crack. Mrs. Turkey's eggs cracked open and out came some little spotted turkeys.

(Turn cluster over.)

Finally, all the cracking noise woke Easter Rabbit.

(Stand rabbit upright.)

"Oh, dear me," he said. "Whatever will I do? It is time to deliver Easter eggs to the children and now I have no eggs." He thought and thought.

Quickly Easter Rabbit gathered the chicks, ducklings, and turkeys.

(Have rabbit gather the clusters.)

"No eggs this year," he said. "This Easter the boys and girls will get surprises in their Easter baskets." And away he hopped with the chicks, ducklings, and turkeys.

(Hop rabbit, carrying animals, off the board.)

What do you think the children will find in their Easter baskets?

(Wait for answer.)

Make 5

FlannelGraphs reproducible page, copyright © 1986 David S. Lake Publishers

A Birthday Cake for Me   45

White

Red

Red
(make 3)

Black

Yellow

Blue
(make 4)

Red
(make 2)

Pink

FlannelGraphs reproducible page, copyright © 1986 David S. Lake Publishers

FlannelGraphs reproducible page, copyright © 1986 David S. Lake Publishers

Blue Ribbon Winners   47

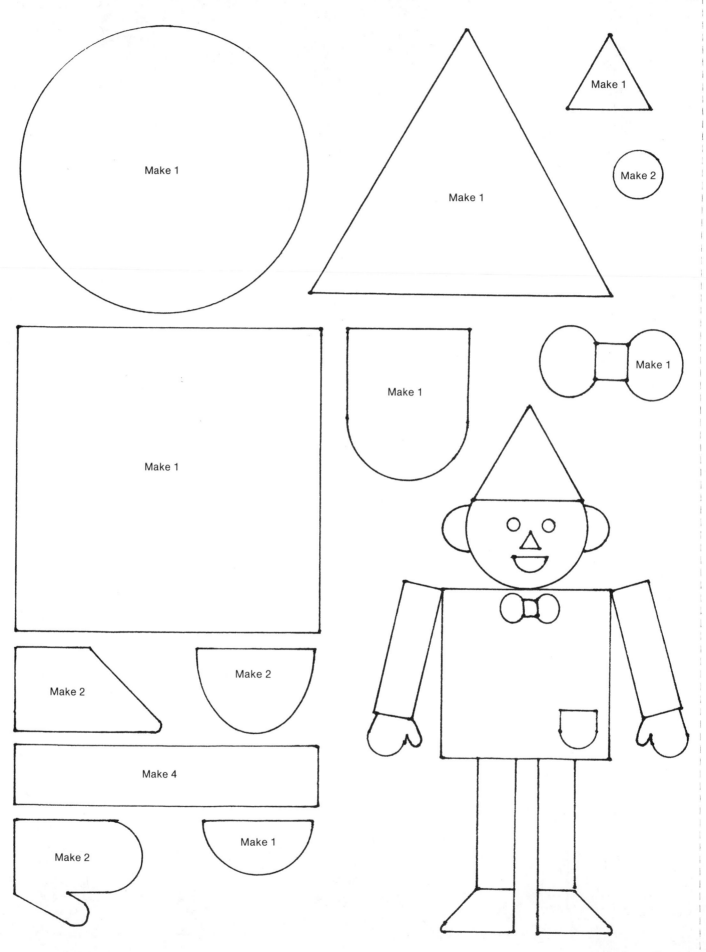

Make 1

Make 1

Make 1

Make 2

Make 1

Make 1

Make 1

Make 1

Make 2

Make 2

Make 4

Make 2

Make 1

FlannelGraphs reproducible page, copyright © 1986 David S. Lake Publishers

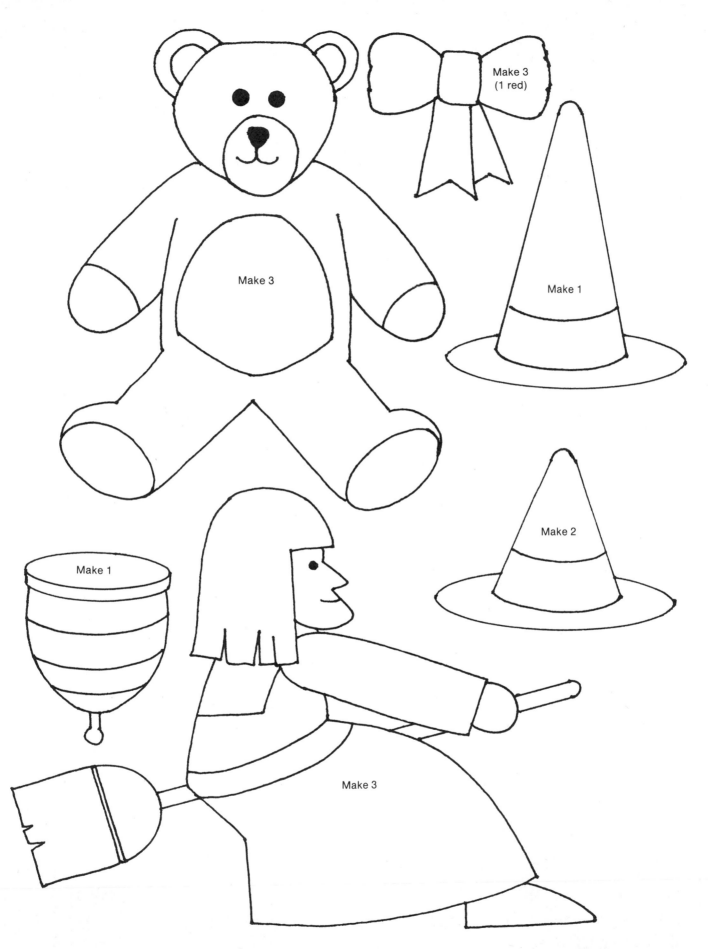

Make 3
(1 red)

Make 1

Make 3

Make 2

Make 1

Make 3

FlannelGraphs reproducible page, copyright © 1986 David S. Lake Publishers

Make 3

Make 2

Make 2

Cap A

Cap B

Make 1

Cap C

- For "same size" activity, make 2 Cap Bs and 1 Cap A.
- For "same color" activity, make 3 Cap Bs, one a different color.

- For "same shape" activity, make 2 Cap Bs and 1 Cap C.

FlannelGraphs reproducible page, copyright © 1986 David S. Lake Publishers

FlannelGraphs reproducible page, copyright © 1986 David S. Lake Publishers

Discovering Opposites   51

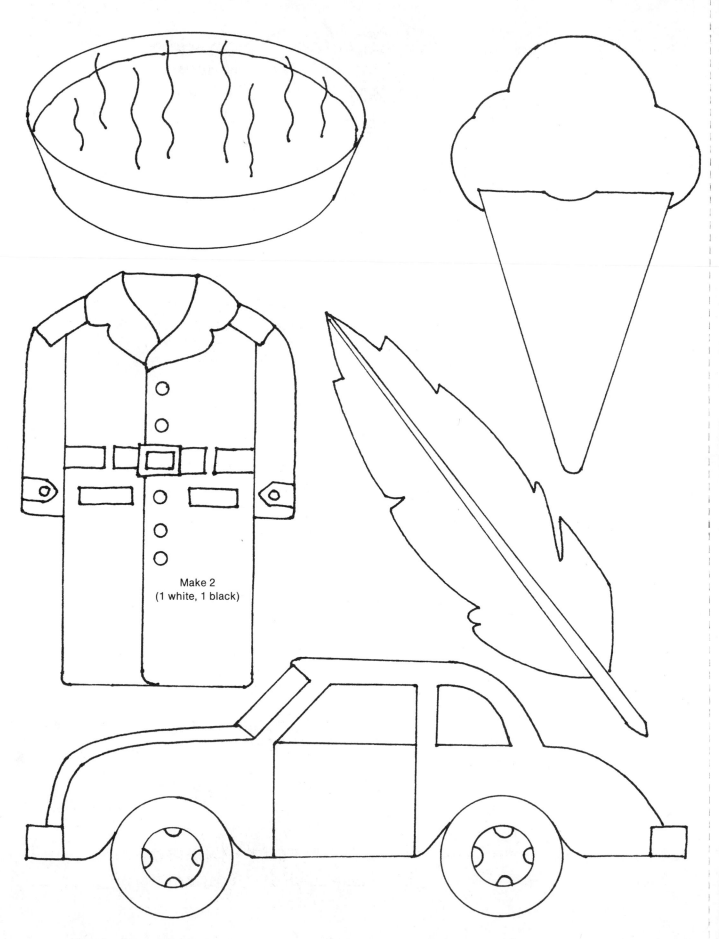

Make 2
(1 white, 1 black)

FlannelGraphs reproducible page, copyright © 1986 David S. Lake Publishers

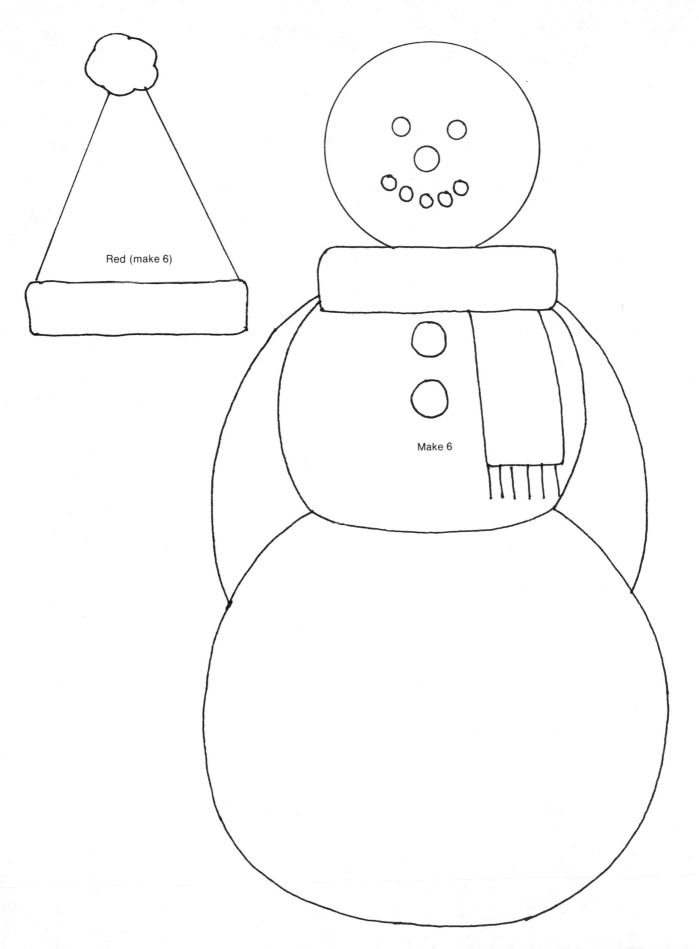

Red (make 6)

Make 6

FlannelGraphs reproducible page, copyright © 1986 David S. Lake Publishers

Six Little Snowpeople   53

FlannelGraphs reproducible page, copyright © 1986 David S. Lake Publishers

Make 4

Make 4

FlannelGraphs reproducible page, copyright © 1986 David S. Lake Publishers

Four Happy Clowns   55

Make 4

Make 6

Make 5

FlannelGraphs reproducible page, copyright © 1986 David S. Lake Publishers

Glue a different number of black spots on the back
of each ladybug.

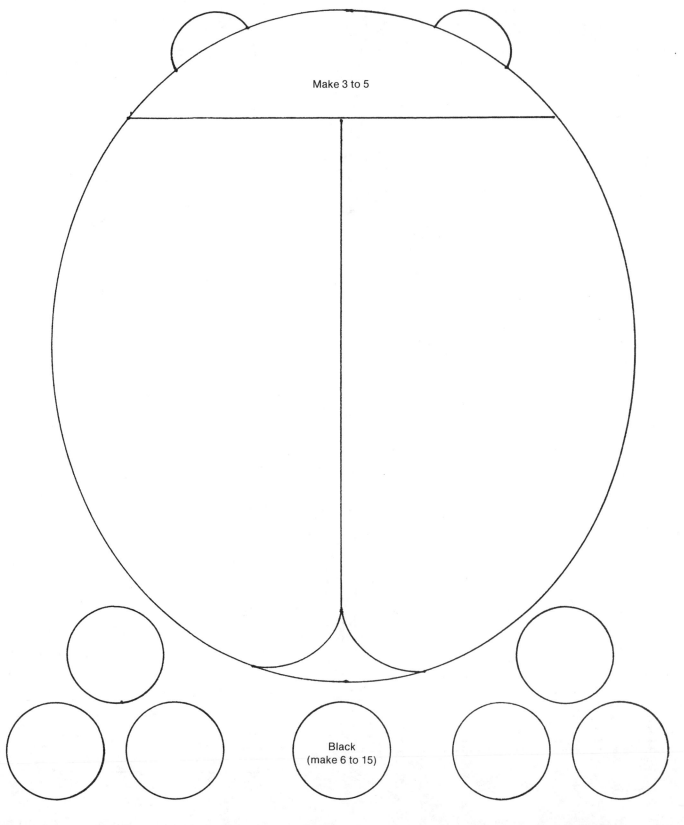

Make 3 to 5

Black
(make 6 to 15)

FlannelGraphs reproducible page, copyright © 1986 David S. Lake Publishers

FlannelGraphs reproducible page, copyright © 1986 David S. Lake Publishers

Make 3
(1 red, 1 yellow,
1 green)

FlannelGraphs reproducible page, copyright © 1986 David S. Lake Publishers

Stop and Go Light   59

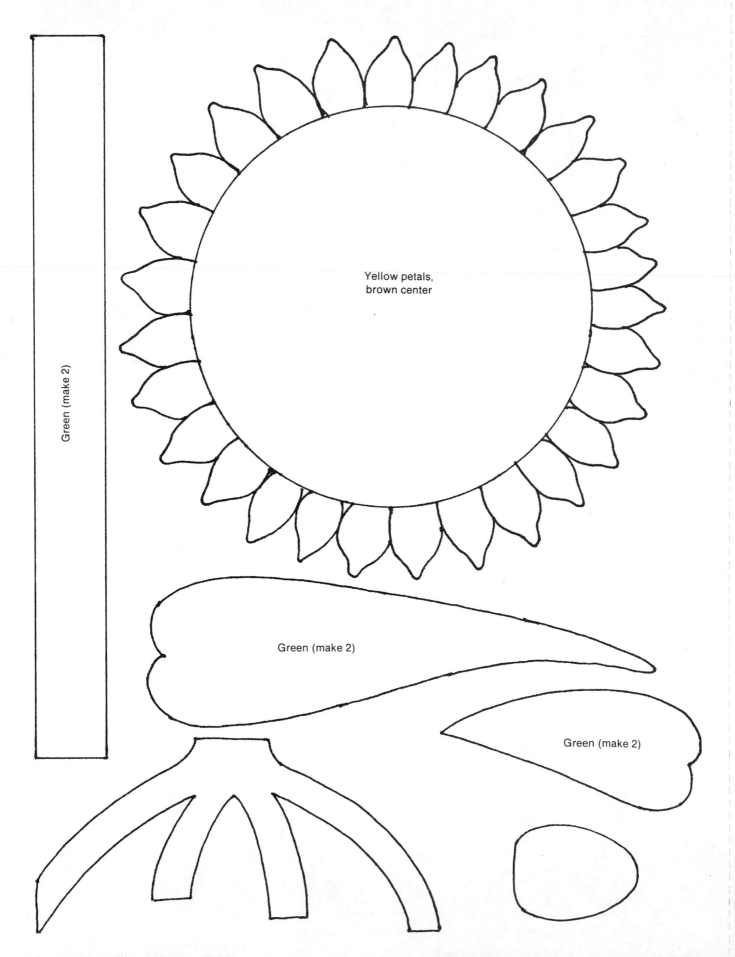

Green (make 2)

Yellow petals,
brown center

Green (make 2)

Green (make 2)

FlannelGraphs reproducible page, copyright © 1986 David S. Lake Publishers

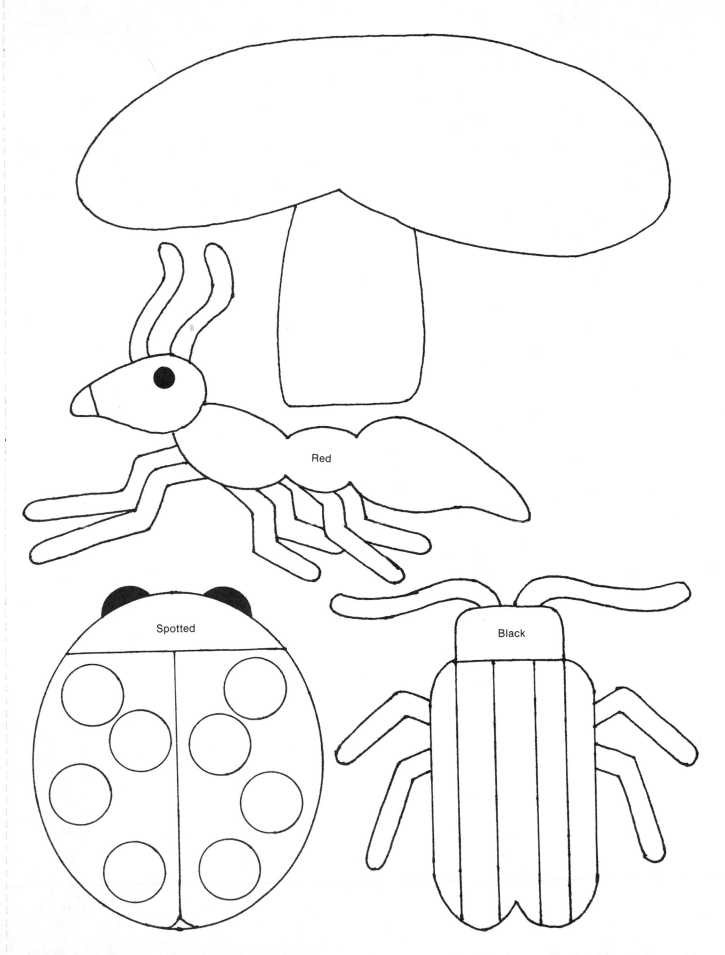

Red

Spotted

Black

White

Green

Yellow

FlannelGraphs reproducible page, copyright © 1986 David S. Lake Publishers

Redheaded

Gray

Brown

FlannelGraphs reproducible page, copyright © 1986 David S. Lake Publishers

Olie and the Cloud   63

Green

FlannelGraphs reproducible page, copyright © 1986 David S. Lake Publishers

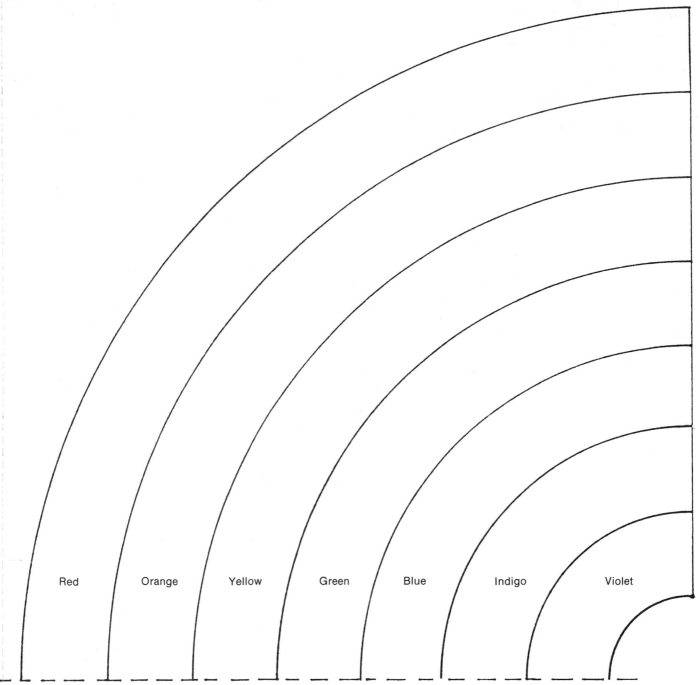

Red   Orange   Yellow   Green   Blue   Indigo   Violet

Fold Pelon, and place this line on fold.

FlannelGraphs reproducible page, copyright © 1986 David S. Lake Publishers

Seven Beautiful Colors   65

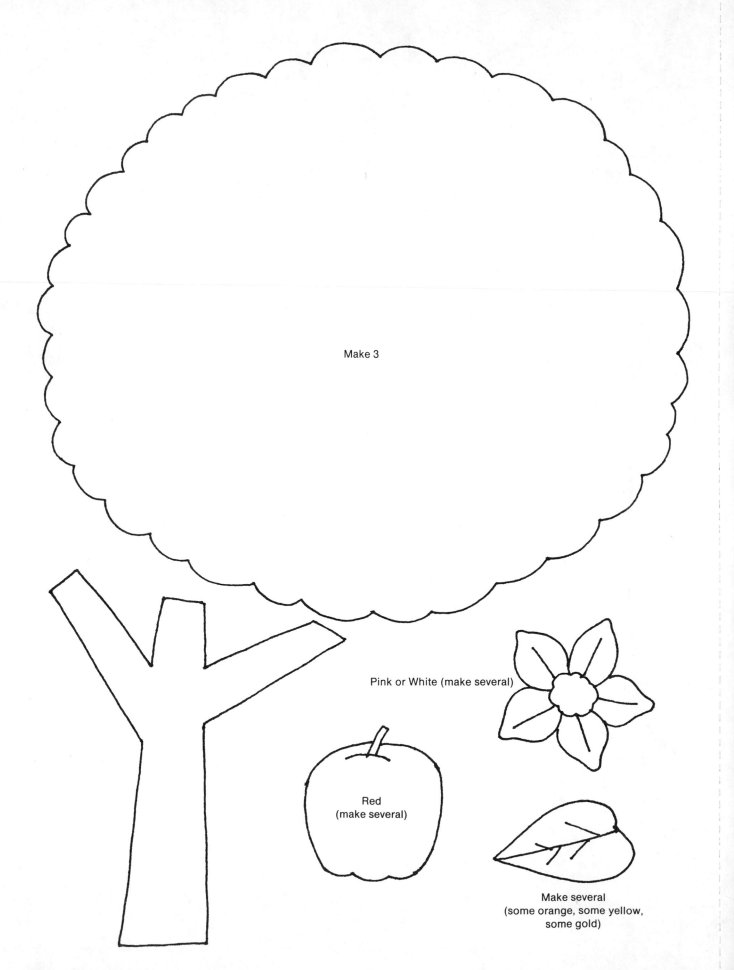

Make 3

Pink or White (make several)

Red
(make several)

Make several
(some orange, some yellow,
some gold)

66   A Special Tree

FlannelGraphs reproducible page, copyright © 1986 David S. Lake Publishers

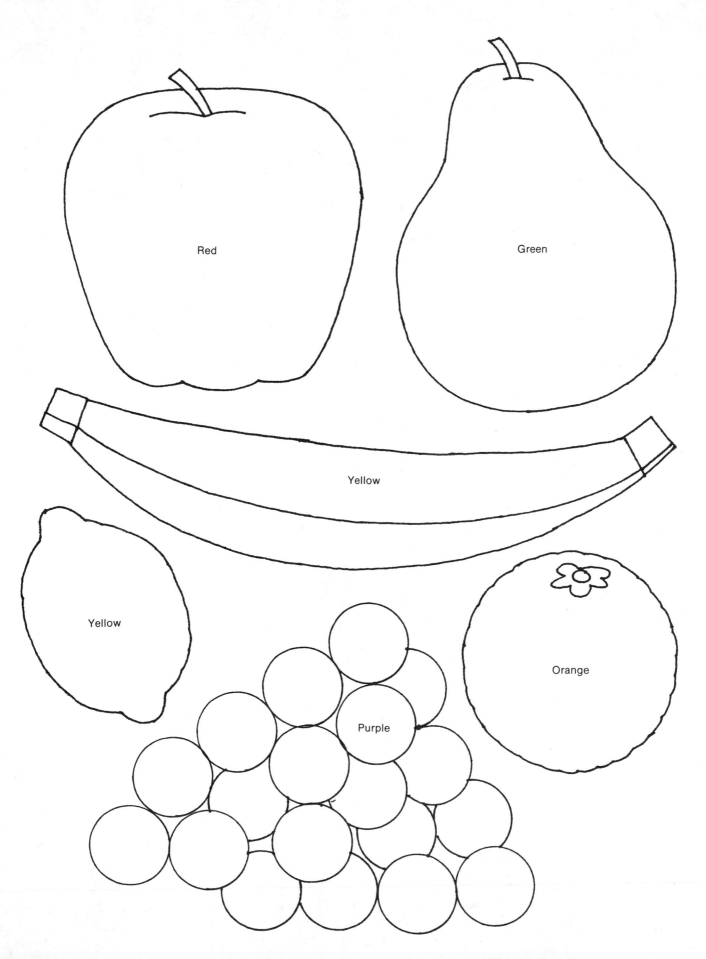

Red

Green

Yellow

Yellow

Purple

Orange

FlannelGraphs reproducible page, copyright © 1986 David S. Lake Publishers

The Happy Fruit Tree   67

FlannelGraphs reproducible page, copyright © 1986 David S. Lake Publishers

Black

FlannelGraphs reproducible page, copyright © 1986 David S. Lake Publishers

The Rollaway Snowperson   69

Make 5 (1 blue,
1 yellow, 1 orange,
1 black, 1 brown)

Orange

Yellow

Brown

Black dress

FlannelGraphs reproducible page, copyright © 1986 David S. Lake Publishers

Make several

Red

FlannelGraphs reproducible page, copyright © 1986 David S. Lake Publishers

The Witch Who Couldn't Fly   71

Make several

White

Red
(make 3)

FlannelGraphs reproducible page, copyright © 1986 David S. Lake Publishers

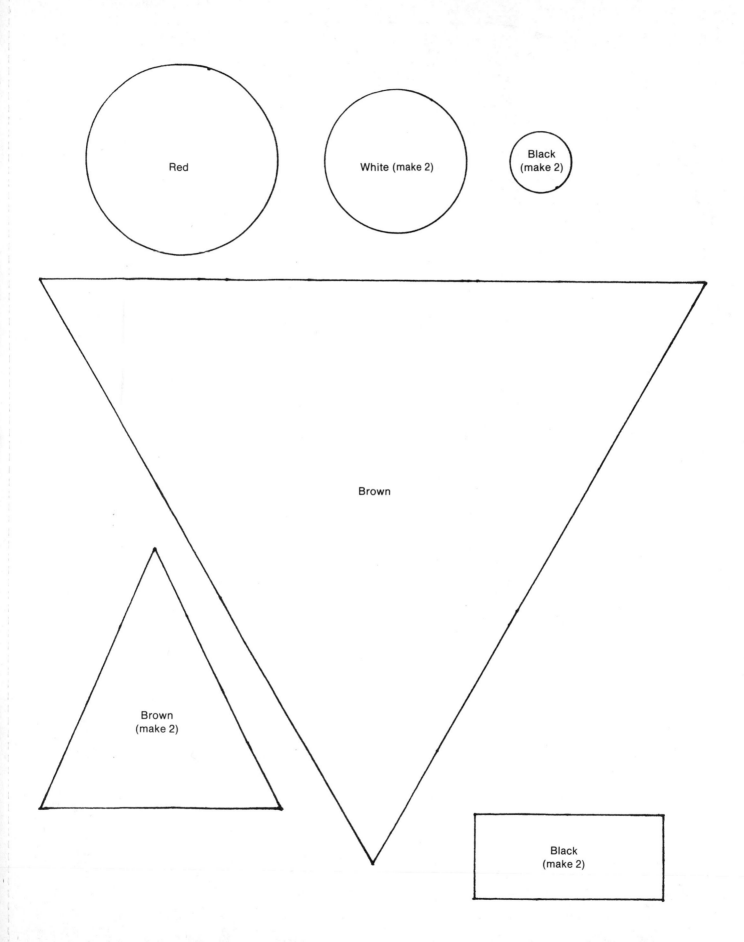

Red

White (make 2)

Black (make 2)

Brown

Brown (make 2)

Black (make 2)

FlannelGraphs reproducible page, copyright © 1986 David S. Lake Publishers

Make 2 for double thickness

Pink

Make 2 (1 decorated, 1 gold)

Yellow

Yellow

Brown

White

FlannelGraphs reproducible page, copyright © 1986 David S. Lake Publishers

Make 3 (1 brown,
1 white, 1 speckled)

FlannelGraphs reproducible page, copyright © 1986 David S. Lake Publishers

FlannelGraphs reproducible page, copyright © 1986 David S. Lake Publishers